REFLECT

Christ-Centered Design

Discover Purpose

WHEATON PRESS

READ. RESPOND. REFLECT.

REFLECT: CHRIST-CENTERED DESIGN

Published in the U.S. by Wheaton Press
www.wheatonpress.com

For more books in this series, classroom and small group discounts, and other resources, visit www.wheatonpress.com.

ISBN-13: 978-0615764719
ISBN-10: 0615764711

For Jesus, who graciously invites all of us
to rediscover our divine design.

CONTENTS

INTRODUCTION

We Were Created for a Purpose

Have you ever stopped to wonder what your purpose in life really is? Have you ever marveled at the riddle of life, or the mystery of death, and felt there must be a reason for it all?

The Christian faith presents a view of life that is both holistic and purposeful. In the Scriptures, we learn that the purpose of this created world is to reflect the creativity, love, and majestic power of the Creator. All of creation is magnificent. However, there is something uniquely important about humans. We are made in the Creator's own image. Our purpose, therefore, is to reflect the character of the Creator and to honor Him through our lives and our relationship with the rest of creation.

But many of us never stop to consider the amazing ramifications of our design. We care only for our own happiness and self-interest. Our lives reflect these selfish, small-minded priorities instead of the original grand purpose for which we were designed.

We all have stories of how our lives have veered off course and fallen short of God's ideal. We make choices that cause the image of the Creator, which should be evident in our lives, to instead become distorted and unrecognizable. Ironically, even our most well-intentioned efforts to live in a good, meaningful way often result in smearing more "grime" across the surface of our lives.

But here's the good news: no matter what your life looks like, no matter how messed up it is, no matter how far away from your original purpose you find yourself right now, each of us has an opportunity to accept the Creator's invitation to return to the purpose for which He created us. We are invited to return to our original calling and to live out the joy and fullness of our divine design.

In the Bible, the apostle Paul clearly says we are called to return to our created purpose and to become imitators of our perfect God. But who is this Creator God we are called to imitate? And how is it possible for us to return to our divine design? Those questions are what this book is about.

CHAPTER 1

CREATED
TO REFLECT

The Image of God

You are valuable—not because of anything you've done, and not because of any skill or talent you possess, but because of the one who created you and the purpose you were created to fulfill. Did you know you are a masterpiece created by the greatest artist in the universe? You are designed to reflect the artist's character, wisdom, and majesty.

While describing God's creation of the world, the first book of the Bible says this about the creation of humanity:

"Then God said, 'Let us make man in our image, after
our likeness. And let them have dominion over the
fish of the sea and over the birds of the heavens and
over the livestock and over all the earth and over every
creeping thing that creeps on the earth.'
"So God created man in his own image,
  in the image of God he created him;
  male and female he created them."

- Genesis 1:26–27, ESV

When God created humans, He made them in His image.
This means we were created to be like our maker. This is
God's unique intent for our design: that we would reflect
Him. This concept is the doctrine of the *Imago Dei*—that we
were endowed by our Creator with the special quality and
responsibility of being like God and representing Him.

**God made you. He created you as a reflection of
His image. You belong to Him in body and spirit.**

David—a songwriter, shepherd, and one of the earliest
kings over the nation of Israel—wrote a famous hymn that
marvels at God's intimate presence and involvement with His
people. When describing God's role in his life, David writes:

> "For it was you who formed my inward parts;
> you knit me together in my mother's womb.
> I praise you, for I am fearfully and wonderfully made.
> Wonderful are your works;
> that I know very well."
>
> - Psalm 139:13-14, NRSV

This psalm is a beautiful reminder of the incredible care and craftsmanship the master artist invests in each of His children. Even before we are born, we are "knit together" and are "wonderful" works of God.

Job, a man whose story is recorded in the book of the Bible named after him, also described God's creative involvement in human life when he said:

> "You clothed me with skin and flesh,
> and knit me together with bones and sinews."
>
> - Job 10:11, ESV

Fearfully and Wonderfully

I don't know about you, but the idea of God crafting me by hand is a bit overwhelming. The psalmist David, who praised God for "knitting" him in his mother's womb, also says that when God wanted to create the universe, He simply *breathed* the stars into existence!

"By the word of the LORD the heavens were made,
their starry host by the breath of his mouth."
- Psalm 33:6, NIV

Which is more difficult for God—speaking solar systems into existence or knitting individuals together? I don't know. But if both creative actions reflect God's majesty and power, it's humbling to consider that, while it took nothing more than a "breath" for God to create the heavens, He stopped to carefully knit each of us together by hand.

If you're unfamiliar with the art of knitting, here are a few things you should know. Knitters use hundreds of different types of stitches to turn a one-dimensional strand of yarn into two-dimensional fabric. They accomplish this by creating connecting paths of yarn called "courses." Each course consists of a series of symmetrical loops that travel both above and below the meandering path of the yarn. Each course is designed so it can be stretched in multiple directions.

This allows a knitted garment to fit the unique form of the person it's covering.

The process of knitting involves three basic steps that are repeated, using a variety of methods to produce different effects. While it's possible for some larger garments to be knit together seamlessly, a final product (such as a sweater) is actually made up of thousands of individual stitches that form several unique sections, which are then sewn together to create the whole.

While most knitters use knitting needles (or "knitting pins"), an individual actually needs only his or her fingers to accomplish the entire knitting process in its basic form.

In other words, it is possible for a master knitter to literally handcraft each individual stitch.

This vivid image of the Master Creator handcrafting us, coupled with discoveries in the field of DNA, both paint a picture of the intimate involvement between the Creator and His creation.

Hand-Crafted Masterpiece

The acronym "DNA" stands for "deoxyribonucleic acid."

Over the past 50 years, scientists have been learning that DNA is the microscopic language that forms the basis for all living things.

Similar to knitting, which consists of three basic tasks that are repeated, DNA has four nucleotides that combine with chemicals called amino acids. These are rearranged continuously to form the "stitches" that act like the rungs of a ladder to form the individual parts of every living thing.

The amount of DNA that fits on the head of a pin holds enough information to fill a stack of books from the earth to the moon and back . . . 500 times. Yet even if two people (identical twins, for example) were to have exactly the same DNA, they would still have different fingerprints.[1]

The prophet Isaiah reminds us that the master artist who designed you down to your fingerprints is the same one who spoke the heavens into existence:

> "It is I [God] who made the earth
>   and created mankind on it.
> My own hands stretched out the heavens;
>   I marshaled their starry hosts."
>
> - Isaiah 45:12, NIV

The Heavens Declare

Have you ever sat outside on a summer night and marveled at the stars? Have you ever stood on the brink of the Grand Canyon, or gazed at the beauty of a winter sunset, and felt a twinge of awe at the works of the master Creator? If you've felt this sense of awe, you aren't alone. David wrote:

> "The heavens declare the glory of God,
>   and the sky above proclaims his handiwork."
>   - Psalm 19:1, ESV

In his book *Confessions,* the fourth-century theologian St. Augustine said:

> "Men go abroad to wonder at the heights of mountains, at the huge waves of the sea, at the long courses of the rivers, at the vast compass of the ocean, at the circular motions of the stars, and they pass by themselves without wondering."

Jesus Takes Center Stage

We've been speaking generically about the triune God as Creator, but did you know the Bible specifically describes Jesus' role in creation?

15

The apostle John wrote:

> "Through him all things were made; without him nothing was made that has been made."
>
> - John 1:3, NIV

That means you were handcrafted by the hand of Jesus! The very same Jesus whose handiwork can be seen throughout the heavens is the master artist who knit you together in your mother's womb.

You are infinitely valuable because of Jesus Himself, who handcrafted you for a purpose.

You Are His Masterpiece

A masterpiece is recognized not only for its own merits, but also because it reflects the artist who created it. Art critics and collectors work very carefully to separate forgeries from original works of art. Each work is carefully examined under a microscope to find the particular nuances of the original artist and to ensure each piece's authenticity.[2]

For example, Martin Kemp, an Oxford professor of art history and an esteemed authenticator of the work of Leonardo da Vinci, has the power to send paintings either to the world's greatest museums or to the trash.

Kemp's opinion regarding a piece's authenticity can turn a seemingly worthless scrap of painted canvas into a priceless historical artifact. In the same manner, if Kemp identifies a piece as a forgery, his decision has the power to send that piece into the garbage.

A Monet or Renoir painted by a forger is just another painting. On the other hand, a certain Renoir painting might be *thought* to be a forgery until an authenticator's close examination determines the artist's brushstrokes and technique are indeed Renoir's work. Current art authenticators are so precise that they can identify even the partial swirls of a fingerprint left inadvertently by the artist.

In the same way that a masterpiece can be recognized by its creator's fingerprints, so God's handiwork can be seen in you.

Fingerprints of God

You and I are marked with the fingerprints of God. We don't receive our value because of who we are or what we do, but because of the artist who designed us and whose image we were created to reflect and display.

Our value is not earned. Rather, our value is inherently placed in us by the one who knit us together by hand and marked us with His fingerprints.

Created for Display

Consider this: our inherent value and purpose are two different things. For example, an authenticated masterpiece that is wrapped in brown paper and hidden in a closet is still a valued masterpiece. (It may even be worth more than well-painted forgeries displayed in prestigious galleries.) However, the intention of the artist was not for his or her work of art to be hidden at the back of a closet. The purpose of the masterpiece is for it to be treasured and displayed.

In a similar manner:

You and I were not created to hide the Creator's imprint. We were created to reflect and display the glory of our Creator through our lives.

Paul addresses this idea in his second letter to the Corinthian church. He writes that we are like "jars of clay," displaying the power of our Creator rather than our own power.

"For what we preach is not ourselves . . . But we have this treasure in jars of clay to show that this all-surpassing power is from God and not from us."
- 2 Corinthians 4:5-7, NIV

Visit any art gallery, and you'll notice a card beside each work of art. This card displays the title of the piece and often includes a statement of the artist's purpose for his or her creation.

Each work reflects its creator. Each description carries a revelation of the artist's intent.

The Image of God

In the first chapter of Genesis, God uses this description to reveal His unique intent for our design:

"Then God said, 'Let us make mankind in our image, in our likeness, so that they may rule over the fish in the sea and the birds in the sky, over the livestock and all the wild animals, and over all the creatures that move along the ground.'

"So God created mankind in his own image, in the image of God he created them; male and female he created them."
- Genesis 1:26-27, NIV

Saying you and I were created "in the image of God" is very different than saying you and I were created to become litle gods. We belong to God and were not created to become His equals. (Many of us, however, do live our lives apart from God—as if we don't need Him. We value our own desires and plans above God's.)

The Old Testament prophet Malachi exalted the singularity of God and our humble relationship to Him:

> "Has not the one God made you? You belong to him in body and spirit."
>
> - Malachi 2:15a, NIV

God made you. He created you as a reflection of His image. You belong to Him in both body and spirit.

But for What Purpose and What Intent?

In Paul's letter to the early church in Ephesus, God reveals His design and purpose. To understand the context of Paul's words in Ephesians, it's important to know that in his letter to the church in Corinth, he defined the church not as a *building* but as *individuals* united by salvation in Christ.

"Now you are the body of Christ, and each one of you is a part of it."

- 1 Corinthians 12:27, NIV

Keep that definition of the church in mind as Paul further clarifies the Father's intention and design:

"His intent was that now, through the church, the manifold wisdom of God should be made known to the rulers and authorities in the heavenly realms."

- Ephesians 3:10, NIV

The first time I really grasped the significance of this verse was life-altering. Consider the ramifications as we piece together the puzzle, beginning with the idea that you and I are handcrafted creations of the almighty God. We are literally masterpieces, created by the Master and displayed on a heavenly scale to reflect the wisdom of the One who created us. The earth is our frame, and the heavenly realms are our audience.

Recognizing this truth alters your understanding of purpose. No longer will you exist to bring honor and glory to yourself. Instead, your singular, expressed purpose shifts toward bringing honor and glory to the One who created you, and the One you were created to reflect.

Reflection

1. What ideas or images stood out to you in this chapter?

2. What was encouraging? Why?

3. What was frustrating? Why?

4. Have you ever considered what your life is worth to your Creator? Why or why not?

5. Did this chapter change any of your previously held thoughts or beliefs? How or why?

Consider . . .

"You are valuable—not because of anything you've done, and not because of any skill or talent you possess, but because of the One who created you and the purpose you were created to fulfill. Did you know you are a masterpiece created by the greatest Artist in the universe? You are designed to reflect the Artist's character, wisdom, and majesty."

6. What was your reaction to this statement when you read it at the beginning of the chapter? Do you think it's accurate? Why or why not?

7. In what places have you tried to find value in your life? What has your experience been with those attempts? How have they worked for you? Worked against you? Explain.

8. Would you say your life currently reflects its intended purpose and design? Why or why not?

CHAPTER 2

SEARCHING FOR SIGNIFICANCE

It's strange and sometimes tragic to watch people and objects being used outside of their intended purposes. A butter knife might be the perfect tool for slicing through butter, but it makes a less-than-ideal screwdriver. A baseball player could use a Louisville Slugger to hit a towering, majestic home run, but the same tool could be misused as a weapon of assault.

People often waste their lives trying to become something they can never be. You and I were created for a purpose: to reflect the majesty, wisdom, and character of the One who created us. But many of us are not living according to this intended purpose. Instead of mirroring the One whose image we are designed to reflect, many of our lives reflect our own design, will, and intentions.

God's design for our lives has careened off course into a reflection of something less than His ideal.

Rather than embracing and resting in our divine design, we are discontent with our intended purpose. We question our Creator's motives and His design. We are plagued with questions like "Why them and not me?" and "What if God doesn't want me to be happy?"

But if we're honest with ourselves, we'll admit our actions are often motivated by a craving for happiness and fulfillment. Our lives revolve around pursuits that are attempts to validate our own existence.

iMatter

Some of us seek validation and happiness through a pursuit of excellence. This desire can drive us toward academic awards or sports trophies. It can propel us to land the lead role in a musical or to be accepted into the "right" college. Our accomplishments, however, are motivated by a desire to please others and feel satisfaction.

For others of us, the search for validation impacts our romantic relationships, determines the way we dress and behave, and influences the types of friends we choose.

Our desire to be remembered for something more than "a line on our tombstone" dictates the schools we attend, the jobs we select, and often the relationships we choose to pursue, tolerate, or end.

Social networking is awash with opportunities to seek validation through the attention and approval of others. We post status updates and photos that summarize and glamorize our daily events, publicize our thoughts in tweets, and collect hundreds of online friends and followers. The "likes," retweets, and friend requests validate our uniqueness and make us feel that our thoughts and opinions matter. Some of us also create online petitions and join social movements to feel like we are making a mark on the world.

We can also seek validation by elevating certain people to celebrity status. Popular musicians, Hollywood personalities, novelists, Olympic athletes, politicians, influential pastors and thinkers—these are all types of people whose causes we champion and whose successes we celebrate.

We retweet their comments and analyze everything about them in magazines. We subscribe to their fan pages and fantasize about their lives. We wear their names on our clothes and place their photos on our walls. We long to be like them, to meet them, to date them—or at least to be associated with them in some way.

But celebrity heroes and heroines inevitably disappoint us. They let us down when they demonstrate they are human. Perhaps it's due to a scandal or simply fading out of the picture. Or maybe we merely get tired of them and move on to a new star who is smarter, hotter, or more talented. Whatever the situation, those celebrities fail to provide the long-term meaning we so desperately desire.

So how do we respond? We treat them with scorn, like the disgraced Greek gods of old. We reduce them to objects of our wrath. Scoffing at their misfortune and gossiping about them, we take pride in their reduced status as we begin our search for new heroes to fill the void that remains in our lives. But the way we identify with celebrities will never provide us with the long-term validation or meaningful identity we desperately desire.

Internal Pursuits, Addictions, and Diversions

Some of us have given up the hope of being validated by someone or something outside of ourselves. As a result, we pursue money and other types of material satisfaction in place of relationships. We try to purchase the validation and security that family relationships, friendships, or romantic encounters have failed to provide. If our income is inadequate, we'll often sacrifice our future well-being for present happiness by using credit cards and other schemes that lead us into cycles of debt and result in overcharged lifestyles.

If money doesn't offer an adequate form of escape, we distract ourselves from reality in other ways. Addictions to pornography, video games, television, exercise, food, alcohol, adrenaline, the Internet, and obsessive busyness can all be unhealthy attempts to control our environment or escape the pain of reality.

But our avenues of escape have a way of catching us and returning us to the unpleasant realities we were attempting to escape. Like addicts who long to return to their first high, we risk more and more of our time, money, and relationships— only to continue to experience less than satisfactory results.

The 1980s Generation

While every generation has its own story, perhaps no generation displays the pursuit of something outside ourselves—the desire for something bigger—better than the

1980s, the generation in which I grew up.

Historians say the 1980s was a decade that glorified self-indulgence and the pursuit of all that money could buy. Double-income parents entrusted their children and teens to local shopping malls. These "mall rats," as they were called, spent time and money looking for validation through name-brand shoes, jeans, and sunglasses. Certain name brands grew rich as we bought into their promises to make us happy and validate our existence. Big hair, big music, big radios, and lots of big shoulder pads gave us opportunities to be noticed and to live beyond ourselves.

"Whatever, Dude"

These two words sum up the hangover of apathy following the 1980s era of glorification of stuff, gratification of self, and the pursuit of all that money could buy. In the 1990s, "whatever, dude" was more than a popular phrase. It was the mantra for a generation that had experienced the waning of the previous decade and realized that, when the party was over, we still felt empty.

It was as if an entire generation woke up one Monday morning to face a new week—only to realize our previous week of overtime earnings, designed to create enough money for a weekend of self-indulgent gratification, had already been spent. We were now unsure whether it was worth it to show up for work on Monday morning. Groggy and only partially aware of our epiphany, we eventually rolled out of bed, called in sick to work, and slipped into our most comfortable T-shirt. When faced with the disapproval of parents, bosses, and teachers, we just rolled our eyes and muttered, "Whatever, dude."

My Story

For me, a moment of awakening occurred in my thirties. Struggling with the need to carry out things that would validate my existence, my list of accomplishments was long. The "Awards, Honors, and Achievements" section of my résumé was continually updated . . .

. . . until the day I reached a personal goal I'd sacrificed for and strived to accomplish for years.

Only hours after accomplishing what had been a major finish line in my life, I felt empty. I was taken aback at my lack of internal validation. It took several months for me to be able to articulate an exact emotion. Suffice it to say that, at a relatively young age, I felt tired, old, and puzzled that the accomplishment of my goal left me feeling unfulfilled instead of satisfied. Having crossed my finish line, I was surprised by the internal question, *What next?*

What Next?

Would I decide to continue down my previous path by creating a new set of goals or identifying a new finish line? Would I retire from my pursuits, wrestle through the feelings of emptiness, and hope my previous accomplishments would become their own validation? Or would I empty my hands of my own purposes, intentions, and will for my life and open them to God's purposes, intentions, and will?

Check Your Ladder

Perhaps you've faced a similar moment or wrestled with similar questions. Maybe you've experienced the shock of climbing the rungs of a ladder of accomplishment, only to discover you struggled and sacrificed to reach the top of a ladder that was leaning against the wrong wall.

The pursuit of any goal—no matter how noble or desirable—other than the goal we were designed to accomplish is a pursuit that will end in meaninglessness.

Even a cursory look at our past will uncover these abandoned ladders. Some are abandoned because they represent goals or pursuits never finished. Others represent dreams that, under the harsh realities of life, ended up broken or discarded. Still others lean against the walls of accomplished-but-forgotten goals. The rungs of these ladders are well-worn, since they used to be cherished and receive daily attention. But now they've collected so much dust, it's difficult to tell the difference between those that formerly seemed like the core to our identity and any other ladder we are happy to forget.

When we look even deeper into past pursuits and then examine any ladders we're climbing currently, we may discover a pattern of hard work followed by unsatisfactory results. This pattern—doing the same thing over and over while expecting different results—is what Albert Einstein, the most influential physicist of the previous century, defined as a form of insanity.

Despite this opportunity for personal examination, and despite Einstein's assessment, some of us may still be convinced that reaching the top of our current ladder will give us the satisfaction of a different result.

But Ecclesiastes, an Old Testament book, says otherwise. It's a book of wisdom that examines the ironies and struggles of human life and wrestles through issues of disillusionment and doubt. Ecclesiastes shows that life is meaningless unless it is centered on God. A life centered on God has purpose and significance.

The author of Ecclesiastes reflected on the emptiness of his human pursuits when he wrote:

> "I have seen all the things that are done under the sun;
> all of them are meaningless, a chasing after the wind."
> - Ecclesiastes 1:14, NIV

Whether we recognize it or not, at the core of our insane quest for validation is an attempt to find meaning and happiness in ourselves, instead of embracing God's will and His design for our lives.

If God's purpose for us is to reflect and display His own image, then it doesn't matter how noble or gratifying our priorities may be. All reflect attempts to place our wills above God's will.

For some of us, these attempts to ignore or sidestep God have been out of ignorance. Until now, we were unaware of—or unclear about—God's intentions. For others, it has been a conscious decision to disregard God's will and design in favor of personal desires.

This attitude comes when we, who are created by God, try to ignore or usurp the rightful authority of our Creator.

Regardless of our individual story or the types of walls we've leaned our ladders against, the mere existence of these ladders reveals both the emptiness and consequences of misplaced goals and dreams. Even the ladders to which we find ourselves currently clinging are testaments to our attempts to replace God's design with our own.

Reflection

1. What ideas or images stood out to you in this chapter?

2. What was encouraging? Why?

3. What was frustrating? Why?

4. In what areas of your life have you sought validation in the past?

5. Every time we trade one false pursuit for validation for another false pursuit, we face the insanity of repeating the same process while expecting different results. One of the key quotes in this chapter is:

> "The pursuit of any goal—no matter how noble or desirable—other than the goal we were designed to accomplish is a pursuit that will end in meaninglessness."

Do you agree or disagree? Explain your answer.

CHAPTER 3

SOMETHING HAPPENED IN THE GARDEN

There is, and always has been, a strong tension between humans' desire to live according to God's design for their lives and their desire to live according to their own self-imposed morality (in order to protect their own happiness or self-interest). This struggle between the desire to obey God and the desire to follow one's own way has been a struggle for all God's people in every generation.

Scripture records two pivotal events that illustrate this struggle. These battles of wills both take place in gardens. One garden is recorded in the Old Testament and the other in the New Testament.

The first event took place in the Garden of Eden, the beautiful home God created for Adam and Eve (Gen. 2). In the Garden of Eden, these first humans lived under God's care and protection—dwelling in close relationship with God, nature, and one another. Yet even so, Adam and Eve succumbed to the temptation to make choices that reflected their own desires, instead of trusting in God's ways. Their disobedience proved that they mistrusted God's intentions for their lives; they decided it would be better to take matters into their own hands. They questioned the motivation of God toward them and placed their wills over that of their Creator.

A second battle of wills took place in the Garden of Gethsemane. Jesus spent the night before His death praying in this olive grove near Jerusalem. Knowing He was about to suffer a torturous, humiliating death, He begged His Father to take that "cup of suffering" away from Him . . . if it was possible. Yet, despite His suffering, Jesus concluded with an affirmation of trust and submission to His Father: "Yet I want your will to be done, not mine" (Matt. 26:39b, NLT).

Even when He faced the temptation to choose personal comfort over excruciating pain and death, Jesus chose to trust and glorify His Father rather than taking matters into His own hands. Both of these stories—the story of Adam and Eve's disobedience in the Garden of Eden and the story of Jesus' trust and submission in the Garden of Gethsemane—are examples that have important applications for us today.

The First Garden

As we just explored, the first battle of wills took place in the Garden of Eden and is recorded in the book of Genesis.

This story relates an internal battle over whether Adam and Eve would choose to trust God and live in harmony with His design for their lives, or whether they'd choose to make their own paths in defiance of God's instructions and clearly expressed will.

The word "genesis" simply means "the origin" or "the coming into being of something" (according to the *American Heritage Dictionary*). This first book of the Bible contains the historic account of how God created all things. The opening verses describe the first day of creation:

> "In the beginning, God created the heavens and the earth. The earth was without form and void, and darkness was over the face of the deep. And the Spirit of God was hovering over the face of the waters."
>
> - Genesis 1:1-2, ESV

Throughout the creation account, a pattern emerges: God speaks something into existence and then pronounces it is "good." One of the first things He does is separate light from darkness.

> "And God said, 'Let there be light,' and there was light. And God saw that the light was good. And God separated the light from the darkness. God called the light Day, and the darkness he called Night. And there was evening and there was morning, the first day."
> - Genesis 1:3-5, ESV

Some critics of the Genesis creation account have questioned the claim that God separated light from darkness on the first day of creation and then waited until the fourth day to create the sun, moon, and stars that govern day and night.

> "And God said, 'Let there be lights in the expanse of the heavens to separate the day from the night. And let them be for signs and for seasons, and for days and years, and let them be lights in the expanse of the heavens to give light upon the earth." And it was so. And God made the two great lights—the greater light to rule the day and the lesser light to rule the night— and the stars. And God set them in the expanse of the heavens to give light on the earth, to rule over the day and over the night, and to separate the light from the

darkness. And God saw that it was good. And there
was evening and there was morning, the fourth day."
- Genesis 1:14-19, ESV

This raises an obvious question: how could light, or a day and
night, have existed before the creation of a sun, moon, and
stars? The Bible gives a definite, important explanation.

The apostle John, one of Jesus' twelve disciples and
the author of the Gospel of John, uses the Greek word *logos* as
a title to refer to Jesus Christ. When translated into English,
the term *logos* means "Word."

In the beginning was the Word, and the Word was
with God, and the Word was God. He was in the
beginning with God. All things were made through
him, and without him was not any thing made that was
made. *In him was life, and the life was the light of men.* The
light shines in the darkness, and the darkness has not
overcome it.
- John 1:1-5, ESV (emphasis added)

In these few verses, we learn several incredible things about
Jesus that apply to the question of beginnings and that also
have implications about the purpose of our design.

First, we learn:

**Jesus was not only *with* God in the beginning,
He *was* God from the beginning.**

In other words, there was never a time when God the Father existed when God the Son (Jesus) did not also exist. Jesus' claim to be the incarnate Son of God is made multiple times throughout the historical accounts of His life in the Gospels.

Second, we learn:

Jesus is responsible for all of creation.

Jesus is the Master Artist. He is not the creation; He is the Creator. All things were made through Him, and nothing was made apart from Him.

Third, we learn:

**Jesus brought light to the world
prior to the creation of the sun.**

This is another concept Jesus proclaims with His own words:

"Again Jesus spoke to them, saying, 'I am the light of the world. Whoever follows me will not walk in darkness, but will have the light of life.'"

— John 8:12, ESV

It might seem easy to argue that Jesus was speaking figuratively when He refers to Himself as the "light of the world." After all, Jesus often used stories, parables, and metaphors to make a point. However, there are other passages in the Bible that not only affirm that Jesus was the "light" of the world prior to the creation of the sun, but also that someday, when our present sun and moon are long gone, He will be the light of the new heaven and the new earth. The Old Testament prophet Isaiah writes:

"The sun will be no more your light by day;
    nor will the brightness of the moon give light to
    you,
but Yahweh will be your everlasting light,
    and your God will be your glory."

— Isaiah 60:19, WEB

In a precursor of the full glory of Jesus that was to come, Jesus' disciple Matthew records the story of the Transfiguration of Christ, which occurred during His ministry on Earth.

"He [Jesus] was transfigured before them. His face shone like the sun, and his garments became as white as the light."

- Matthew 17:2, WEB

The apostle Paul had an encounter with the risen Christ on the road to Damascus and was blinded by the *light* of Jesus. Paul later described this life-changing experience when he stood on trial before King Agrippa:

"[A]t noon, O king, I saw on the way a light from the sky, brighter than the sun, shining around me and those who traveled with me."

- Acts 26:13, WEB

The apostle John would later use a similar description for Jesus when describing his vision of the risen Christ:

"His face was like the sun shining at its brightest."

- Revelation 1:16b, WEB

Finally, in the book of Revelation, John tells us the glorified face of Jesus will one day serve as the world's eternal light:

"The city does not need the sun or the moon to shine on it, for the glory of God gives it light, and the Lamb is its lamp."

- Revelation 21:23, NIV

Why Does This Matter?

Three questions are pertinent to our study of God's design for humanity and His desire for our lives to reflect Him.

First, why would God go out of His way to ensure we knew our sun, moon, and stars were not actually created until the fourth day of creation?

Second, what are the implications of Adam and Eve's disobedience in the Garden of Eden?

Third, how do our choices to follow our own desires rather than trust God's will impact God's design for our lives?

#1: Why would God not create the sun until the fourth day?

The answer to this question is best understood when we realize that God designed everything in creation to reflect and worship Him, including the sun, moon, and stars.

"Praise Him, sun and moon!
      Praise Him, all you shining stars!"
                                    - Psalm 148:3, WEB

"From the rising of the sun unto the going down of
the same the Lord's name is to be praised."
                                    - Psalm 113:3, KJV

History shows humans have a propensity to confuse the Creator with His creation.

We take what was initially designed by our Creator to bring glory to Himself, and instead of worshipping our Creator, we worship His creation.

Basically, humans have the tendency to take *good* things and turn them into *god*-things.

A prime example of humanity's tendency to worship creation rather than the Creator can be seen in this partial list of sun gods and goddesses that have been revered throughout the world:

- Amaterasu - Japanese
- Apollo - Greek and Roman
- Helios - Greek god (prior to Apollo)
- Hvar Khshaita - Iranian/Persian
- Liza - West African
- Lugh - Celtic
- Re (Ra) - Egyptian
- Sol - Norse
- Sol Invictus - the unconquered Roman god of the sun
- Surya - Hindu
- Tonatiuh - Aztec
- Utu (Shamash) - Mesopotamian
- Xihe - Chinese

In addition to these external historical references, the Bible also makes internal references to people who chose to worship the sun rather than the God who created the sun:

> "If a man or woman living among you in one of the towns the Lord gives you is found doing evil in the eyes of the Lord your God in violation of his covenant, and contrary to my command has worshiped other gods, bowing down to them or to the sun or the moon or the stars in the sky, and this has been brought to your attention, then you must investigate it thoroughly."
>
> - Deuteronomy 17:2-4a, NIV

It's clear that God finds the worship of the sun, moon, or stars to be a violation of His relational covenant with His people. Many years later, the prophet Ezekiel would describe this same form of evil and misplaced worship when he recorded a vision of men practicing sun-worship in the Lord's temple in Jerusalem:

> "He brought me into the inner court of Yahweh's house; and see, at the door of Yahweh's temple, between the porch and the altar, were about twenty-five men, with their backs toward Yahweh's temple, and their faces toward the east; and they were worshiping the sun toward the east."
>
> - Ezekiel 8:16, WEB

Did you catch that? There, in the inner court of the temple, 25 men had literally turned their backs to their Creator in order to worship His creation.

In the next verse, the Spirit of God says to Ezekiel:

> "He said to me, 'Have you seen this, son of man? Is it a trivial matter for the people of Judah to do the detestable things they are doing here?'"
>
> - Ezekiel 8:17a, NIV

Clearly, God considers it a "detestable" practice to give the praise and glory that rightfully belong to Him to any of His creation. So perhaps one of the key reasons God chose not to create the sun, moon, and stars until the fourth day was so there wouldn't be any confusion between the true light of the world (Jesus) and the lights He designed and created.

#2: What are the implications of what happened in the Garden of Eden between Adam, Eve, and God?

Remember back in the Garden, when we said that a pattern emerged of God creating something and then declaring it was "good"? On the sixth day of creation, God created humankind as the culmination of His creation. God then declared all He had made was *very good.*

> "God saw all that he had made, and it was very good. And there was evening, and there was morning—the sixth day."
>
> - Genesis 1:31, NIV

God also gives Adam and Eve instructions on how to live and interact with the rest of His creation.

"Then God said, 'I give you every seed-bearing plant on the face of the whole earth and every tree that has fruit with seed in it. They will be yours for food. And to all the beasts of the earth and all the birds in the sky and all the creatures that move along the ground—everything that has the breath of life in it—I give every green plant for food.' And it was so."

- Genesis 1:29-30, NIV

A few verses later, we are told that Adam and Eve have the freedom to eat from any tree—except one.

"And the LORD God commanded the man, 'You are free to eat from any tree in the garden; but you must not eat from the tree of the knowledge of good and evil, for when you eat from it you will certainly die.'"

- Genesis 2:16-17, NIV

God's instructions are straightforward, loving, and permissive. There were many wonderful trees that Adam and Eve were free to enjoy in the Garden.

Scripture doesn't tell us how much time passes between the end of chapter two and the beginning of chapter three, yet one thing is clear: Adam and Eve's lives in the garden take a dramatic turn when a tempter—described as a shrewd serpent—addresses Eve. The tempter twists God's words and incites Eve to question God's intentions.

"He said to the woman, 'Did God really say, "You must not eat from any tree in the garden"?'"
                                                    - Genesis 3:1b, NIV

Notice how the Serpent distorts God's words in order to draw Eve away from God. God had explicitly said the humans could eat from any tree in the garden except one, yet the tempter's crafty wording makes Eve question not only God's will, but His intentions for her. The Serpent moves from misquoting God's words to casting doubt on God's motives.

"'You will not certainly die,' the serpent said to the woman. 'For God knows that when you eat from it your eyes will be opened, and you will be like God, knowing good and evil.'"
                                                    - Genesis 3:4-5, NIV

As you read the words "be like God," recognize how they are a perversion of the purpose for which humans were created.

The words of the Serpent in Genesis are noticeably similar to words later written by the prophet Isaiah and credited to the king of Babylon.

"You said in your heart,
    'I will ascend to the heavens;

> I will raise my throne
>> above the stars of God;
> I will sit enthroned on the mount of assembly,
>> on the utmost heights of Mount Zaphon.
> I will ascend above the tops of the clouds;
>> I will make myself like the Most High.'"
>
> — Isaiah 14:13-14, NIV

Scholars differ in opinion as to whether the person speaking in this passage is only the king of Babylon, or whether it's a dual reference to both a human king and to Satan himself. Either way, note how the five statements that begin with the words "I will" carry the same sentiment as the misleading promises made by the Serpent in the Garden. The rebellious, self-centered desires behind these statements are obvious.

But before we point fingers in judgment at Eve or anyone else, it's wise to examine our own hearts. How often have we struggled with the choice between trust and rebellion—between submitting ourselves to God and supplanting His will by placing our desires above His?

Just like Eve, we feel the tension between submitting to God's way and trusting His design for our lives versus rejecting His way and trusting our own design for our lives.

Many objects we find desirable are pleasing to our eyes—just as the fruit of the knowledge of good and evil seemed "pleasing" to Eve.

> "When the woman saw that the fruit of the tree was good for food and pleasing to the eye, and also desirable for gaining wisdom, she took some and ate it. She also gave some to her husband, who was with her, and he ate it."
>
> - Genesis 3:6, NIV

Marketing executives understand Eve's conundrum and capitalize on this human tendency by creating ad campaigns based on the universal human desire for "forbidden fruit." That's why advertisements focus more on selling a lifestyle—or a product's perceived ability to give people greater control over their lives—than they focus on the products themselves.

In a similar way, Satan cunningly persuaded Eve by convincing her that disregarding God would not only result in greater control over her own life, but that the benefits of her choice would be worth the cost.

If we are merely ignorant of God's will, we may justify our decisions by saying we don't really understand His will. Or if we do clearly understand God's will, we may openly defy His ways in preference for our own. But in either scenario, the enemy of God will typically incite our mistrust by making us question God's intentions: "Does God *really* have your best interests at heart?"

#3: How does the choice to replace God's will with our own impact His overall design for our lives?

The Book of Exodus describes how God gave His Law to Moses, the leader of the Israelites. On a mountain called Sinai, Moses had an encounter with God that exceeded any normal human experience.

> "When Moses came down from Mount Sinai, with the two tablets of the testimony in his hand as he came down from the mountain, Moses did not know that the skin of his face shone because he had been talking with God."
>
> - Exodus 34:29, ESV

A few verses later, we learn Moses's face was shining so brightly that he actually had to cover his face with a veil so he didn't terrify all the people!

Consider this: the type of closeness and conversation with God described in this story was astonishing and frightening for the Israelites, yet it had once been entirely natural for Adam and Eve.

Before Adam and Eve tried to elevate themselves above God and defy His will for their lives, it was normal for humans to be in God's presence and to reflect His glory.

The apostle Paul makes reference to the veil of Moses when he writes that those who turn to Christ will be able to contemplate and reflect the glory of God with unveiled faces.

> "And we all, who with unveiled faces contemplate the Lord's glory, are being transformed into his image with ever-increasing glory, which comes from the Lord, who is the Spirit."
>
> - 2 Corinthians 3:18, NIV

Gardens of Gods

The experience of Moses seems foreign to us, because it's difficult to enter God's presence when we question His intentions toward us.

Just like Adam and Eve, we exchange the light of His plan and design for the darkness of our own desires.

Our hearts echo the "I will" statements in our quest to rule our own lives and make ourselves equal to our Creator.

Turning our backs on God, we reject His will and design to instead embrace a variety of "gods" who we think will bring light to our lives.

When we question God's intentions toward us and turn our backs on God, we are listening to the voice of the Enemy. The moment we choose our own desires over God's will and determine to follow a god of our own creation, we join ranks with the Serpent and the king of Babylon as enemies of God and as a result we experience a blinding to the glory of God.

"As for you, you were dead in your transgressions and sins, in which you used to live when you followed the ways of this world and of the ruler of the kingdom of the air, the spirit who is now at work in those who are disobedient."

- Ephesians 2:1-2, NIV

"For, as I have often told you before and now tell you again even with tears, many live as enemies of the cross of Christ. Their destiny is destruction, their god is their stomach, and their glory is in their shame. Their mind is set on earthly things."

- Philippians 3:18-19, NIV

"The god of this age has blinded the minds of unbelievers, so that they cannot see the light of the gospel that displays the glory of Christ, who is the image of God."

- 2 Corinthians 4:4, NIV

Consider the implications of what it means that our hearts have become darkened and our minds have been blinded to the glory of God. Not only are we not participating in the purpose for which we were created but according to these verses apart from a dramatic intervention we can't even see it.

Reflection

1. What ideas or images stood out to you in this chapter?

2. What was encouraging? Why?

3. What was frustrating? Why?

4. God separated light from darkness before creating the sun, moon, and stars. Had you ever noticed that statement before? What are your thoughts on why that is specifically stated in the Book of Genesis?

5. In what ways is Jesus described as the light of the world?

6. What would it be like for your life to reflect the light of Christ? Take a few minutes to write your thoughts.

7. What are some areas of your life where you have traded the light of Jesus for the darkness of other gods?

8. How has placing your will above God's will—or following your own desires instead of trusting His direction in these areas—worked out for you? Explain.

9. What do you think God's intentions are for your life? What experiences have directed you to these conclusions?

CHAPTER 4

GOOD INTENTIONS AND DIRTY RAGS

Our lives, past and present, are checkered with good intentions: projects we intend to finish, books we intend to read, thank-you cards we intend to write, relationships we intend to reconcile, exercise habits we intend to improve, or eating habits we intend to change. Each year we use New Year's Day as an excuse to formalize these good resolutions.

But not all intentions are good. Many of us have suffered because of others' bad intentions and behaviors. Maybe you've been disappointed or hurt by those who promised to care for you and protect your best interests. Perhaps someone who once expressed good intentions toward you ended up lying to you, back-stabbing you, or abusing you. Sometimes this type of experience can make it difficult to trust people who say they have your best interests at heart.

However, if we really stop to consider our own lives, we must acknowledge that our own intentions and actions are often selfish instead of loving, and that we frequently place our own interests ahead of the interests of others. Maybe you have feigned friendliness toward someone or initiated a relationship because you saw closeness with someone as an opportunity to "get ahead" in some way—even if it required taking advantage of that person. Recent statistics show that a large percentage of Americans admit to cheating on a spouse or significant other, taking advantage of co-workers or customers, or lying on tax documents.

The truth is, many of our intentions are *not* good. As a result, we look suspiciously on other people's intentions in order to protect ourselves from being hurt. One of the most interesting aspects of the Serpent's conversation with Eve in Genesis 3 is his insinuation that God had purposefully withheld the very best from Adam and Eve, that their lives were not complete as a result, and therefore, God's intentions toward them might not be as pure as they had assumed.

Ignorance Was Bliss

Have you ever considered that, up until that first moment of self-will, Adam and Eve were ignorant of evil? Until that moment, they knew only the goodness of God and the wholeness of creation. Their bodies were healthy and perfect. In their relationships with each other and with God, Adam and Eve enjoyed perfect love, trust, and unity.

Adam didn't need to frequent the gym after long days of work in order to speed up his aging metabolism. Eve was never self-conscious about her body, and she never worried that Adam would leave her for another woman. They lived lives that were full, complete, and abundant. Neither feared sickness or death. Instead, they experienced the fruits of God's Spirit in their lives and relationships and the goodness of the world that God had given them to cultivate and enjoy.

Imagine a life where you knew and experienced only the fruit of the Spirit: love, joy, peace, patience, kindness, goodness, faithfulness, gentleness, and self-control (Gal. 5:22-23). Imagine a world with no war or violence, no hatred or abuse, no shame, no jealousy, no adultery, no poverty—and no death. There is no need for locks, keys, or security precautions. Instead of living in fear, all people live with perfect trust in one another and in God. This was the way of life God intended. This was the type of life Adam and Eve enjoyed in the Garden.

And yet the Serpent planted a seed of doubt in Adam and Eve's minds by encouraging them to question the trustworthiness of the Creator's motives. These seeds of doubt caused Adam and Eve to desire the one thing that God had warned them against. This desire grew into distrust and enmity toward their Creator.

Questionable Motives

Once we cross that line and begin to question God's motives toward us, it's relatively easy to begin asking questions such as:

> **"Why should I submit to God's will if I don't know whether I trust His intentions toward me?"**

> **"Why shouldn't I sit on the throne of my own life and live by my own rules—especially since my way seems more pleasurable and desirable?"**

Isn't that exactly the situation Adam and Eve found themselves in? These two individuals had known only the goodness of God and were blessed with perfect bodies, perfect relationships, and perfect freedom. Yet they began to question whether or not they were truly loved by the God who had met their every need. They began to wonder if, given the opportunity, they could somehow do it better. Adam and Eve responded by questioning God's motives toward them and by pursuing their desire to become their own gods.

Sound Familiar?

Perhaps it does sound familiar, because we experience the same tension Adam and Eve did. Every day we wrestle with the desire to trust and honor God and the desire to follow our own ideas. Who among us is not guilty of questioning the Creator's motives? Questioning whether He truly heard our prayers? Whether He really cares?

After all, we think, *if God really does care about me, why won't He give me the good things I need? Why won't He give me the friends or happy family I want so desperately? The boyfriend/girlfriend? The husband or wife? The good health? The right test score? Doesn't He care?*

How many times have we questioned God's goodness because He didn't provide us *what* we wanted, *when* we wanted it, or *how* we wanted it?

At some point, we have all turned our backs on God by choosing to put our own desires on the throne of our lives. After all, our way often seems safer than God's will—or maybe just more rewarding, more ambitious, and more fun.

For some of us, choosing our own way instead of God's way might mean pursuing a certain friendship or dating relationship, even though we know that relationship is not in line with God's expressed will for our lives.

For others, it may mean continuing in certain jobs or activities that don't honor God, remaining silent when we should have the courage to speak out, or acting disrespectfully toward people God has commanded us to love. It may mean running headlong into a decision or purchase—determined that we must have what we want, regardless of the cost.

When we examine the track record of our desires and God's failure to respond according to our specifications, our reasons to question His design, goodness, and authority seem solid. So we make our choice. Rebelling against His authority as our Creator, we unapologetically disregard His will. Like spoiled children taking a more "desirable" route toward our own comforts, pleasures, and aspirations, we do whatever it takes to ensure our lives are reflections of our own desires and design—sometimes at great cost to ourselves or those around us.

James, Jesus' brother, speaks of this process in the fourth chapter of the New Testament book that bears his name:

> "Where do you think all these appalling wars and quarrels come from? Do you think they just happen? Think again. They come about because you want your own way, and fight for it deep inside yourselves. You lust for what you don't have and are willing to kill to get it. You want what isn't yours and will risk violence to get your hands on it.

> "You wouldn't think of just asking God for it, would you? And why not? Because you know you'd be asking for what you have no right to. You're spoiled children, each wanting your own way."
>
> - James 4:1-3, MSG

Like gravity, the pursuit of our own way has inevitable consequences. For some of us, it has meant climbing that ladder, only to reach the top and face emptiness instead of fulfillment. For others, it has meant following selfish desires that have resulted in broken relationships, ruined finances, or lost opportunities. Instead of finding joy and freedom, we become enslaved by the very things we thought would bring us life. We experience the pain of watching dreams, careers, or even relationships die as a result of our pursuit of the very things we thought would bring us freedom.

The apostle Paul explores human brokenness when he writes that, while our choices were designed to gratify our cravings, they left us in a position of spiritual death.

> "As for you, you were dead in your transgressions and sins, in which you used to live when you followed the ways of this world and of the ruler of the kingdom of the air, the spirit who is now at work in those who are disobedient. All of us also lived among them at one time, gratifying the cravings of our flesh and following its desires and thoughts. Like the rest, we were by nature deserving of wrath."
>
> - Ephesians 2:1-3, NIV

The Bible uses the term "sin" to describe the act of stepping outside the will of God for our lives. According to Paul's letter to the church in Rome, every person has, at one time or another, stepped outside of God's will and fallen short of His glory.

> "[F]or all have sinned and fall short of the glory of God."
>
> - Romans 3:23, NIV

To understand the implications of Paul's words regarding sin, we don't need to look any further than the keys on our key chains.

Count Your Keys

Most people carry keys. My personal key ring holds my house key, car key, office key, and a few other random keys—I'm not even sure what they open. In addition, I have computer passwords—so many passwords for so many accounts that I have to keep a separate account with a special password simply just to protect all my passwords! Each key and password is a constant reminder that sin exists in our world.

The purpose of a lock or password is to protect something we value from being stolen or misused. The reason we have car keys, computer passwords, window bars, and alarm systems is because we know sin exists. Our keys and passwords are daily reminders to protect ourselves from others who could put their desires above our welfare and sin against us.

The reality of our sinful world was also illustrated through the release of a smartphone with the ability to recognize its owner's unique thumbprint, instead of a word or number-based password. Consider the possibilities of this technology: we won't need passwords anymore!

But within hours of the announcement, news headlines reminded us of the dark possibility that criminals could now have motivation to steal people's *fingers* to access their information. The blogosphere erupted. Instead of reviews analyzing the finer points of the new technology, the dialogue shifted to a debate about which finger would be least problematic for people to lose, should they ever face such grisly criminals.

**Every day we're impacted by the ramifications
of Adam and Eve's decision to respond to God
by sitting on the thrones of their own lives,
thus rebelling against God's will.**

One of the main ramifications is that death entered the world. God's instructions to Adam clearly stated that death would be the consequence of living outside the will of God (Gen. 2:17). In the New Testament, the apostle Paul elaborated on this truth:

"Therefore, just as sin entered the world through one man, and death through sin, and in this way death came to all people, because all sinned."

- Romans 5:12, NIV

Today, you and I are surrounded by the consequences of that decision. Every day, people face the results of death—physical and emotional suffering, relational separation, and the loss of hopes. Every day, people in our world experience sickness, plagues, famine, natural disasters, genocide, and the horrors of war. In my own city, Chicago, people die every weekend from violent crimes—including innocent children whose lives are cut short by stray bullets and other forms of violence.

We face the death of dreams, the death of marriages or other relationships we thought would last forever, and even the "death" of losing homes, memories, abilities, health, and other cherished aspects of life. Because of the pervasiveness of death, we often live in fear. We also experience the fear that results from experiences that have killed our innocence or joy, leaving us feeling dead or numb inside.

Even though we're reminded by the weight of the keys in our pockets and the weight of the pain in our lives, many of us have grown accustomed to the way things are. We've become oblivious to the reality that our lives are only shadows, instead of clear reflections, of the image of God.

Yet there are moments in which we are able to step back from our cycles of self-gratification and efforts to achieve self-validation. In those moments, we look at the empty lives we have created for ourselves and view our choices with regret. Like a foolish shopper who receives a maxed-out credit card statement at the end of a holiday season, we clearly see the consequences of our choices and momentarily gain perspective on our overcharged lives. We wish life had a return policy that would enable us to return our lives back to their original packaging and purpose.

Marred and Muddied

Beneath our brokenness and regret, each of us bear the image of God: in spite of His full reflection being marred and muddied by our rebellious attempts to place our will over His. There are moments in our mud-covered lives where His purpose and design still shine through and allow us to catch glimpses of His character, glory, and purpose. These moments emphasize the ironic truth that sinful and messed-up people are still capable of profound kindness, goodness, and courage.

This double truth is emphasized if we look at the types of stories reported in our daily news. The typical evening news broadcast shares many stories of people who cause harm by choosing self at the expense of others. Whether these stories are accounts of corruption, scandal, war, violence, rape, theft, or the destruction of the environment, selfish acts make up the majority of our news. These discouraging stories are usually followed by a weather forecast, a sports highlight, or a brief "feel-good" story at the end of a broadcast, but stories of true selflessness or righteousness are noticeably rare. The news is a daily reminder of the truth of Paul's words to the Roman Christians:

> "Very rarely will anyone die for a righteous person, though for a good person someone might possibly dare to die."
>
> - Romans 5:7, NIV

Stories in which individuals place the needs of others over their own needs are so rare that our typical response is to hail these people as modern-day heroes, because their actions seem so far outside the norm. Theirs are the few inspiring stories that end our newscasts. These stories are glimmers of hope, reminding us that perhaps we're not all as bad as we seem. Their stories leave us wondering what life would be like if there were a few more heroes like that in our world. We wonder if we would have acted as selflessly under the same circumstances.

Instead of thinking these acts of goodness are self-initiated and make us worthy of praise, the truth is:

Even if we could rely on ourselves to believe enough, be strong enough, try hard enough, or become righteous enough, we could never make ourselves presentable enough to stand before our holy Creator, God.

Left to ourselves, we'd still be relying on our own efforts to regain what we once had: a perfect relationship with our perfect Creator God. The reality is that no amount of personal refinement could make us presentable to Him based on our own merits.

The Old Testament prophet Isaiah summed up our situation:

"All of us have become like one who is unclean,
    and all our righteous acts are like filthy rags;
we all shrivel up like a leaf,
    and like the wind our sins sweep us away."
                                    - Isaiah 64:6, NIV

Dirty Rags

Have you ever tried to clean a mirror with a filthy rag? It doesn't work very well. The grime and grease on the rag will smear the dirt, but the rag won't clean the mirror. The reflected image is smudged and appears increasingly out of focus.

**Beneath our acts of righteousness,
the truth is that we can never fully clean
our reflections while using a dirty rag.**

Even if we could manage to clean ourselves up by our own efforts, without a clear image of God to pattern our lives after, we would continue to pursue our faulty concepts of who God is and what He is like. As a result, we would continue to distort His image under the false impression that we're better off than we actually are.

We must have a clear model of perfection to give us direction and an accurate measurement to determine where we are in the process of growth.

Bad News and Good News

The bad news is this tension between the will of God and the will of man that we saw first in the Garden of Eden ended with human failure. So unless we have a model of what perfection looks like, and we are given an opportunity to receive the type of holistic restoration that transcends our own efforts, we are unable to fix ourselves.

The good news is God has given a perfect model for us to pattern our lives after, and there was a second garden and a second battle of wills that ended with a very different result. This is the source of our hope.

Reflection

1. What ideas or images stood out to you in this chapter?

2. What was encouraging? Why?

3. What was frustrating? Why?

4. When have you suffered because of someone else's selfish intentions? What were the circumstances?

5. How might that negative experience—and others you might have had because of someone's selfish intentions—have influenced your trust in God's intentions for your life? Explain.

6. Where have some of your own intentions led you? What happened as a result?

7. How might your actions be seen as "filthy rags"?

8. In which areas do you find yourself attempting to use filthy rags to remove the effects of sin in your life?

9. After reading this chapter, what are your thoughts about your attempts to fix your own life?

CHAPTER 5

A PERFECT REFLECTION

Our sinfulness does not nullify our calling to reflect the image and glory of God in every area of life. The apostle Paul said it this way: "Therefore, be imitators of God, as dearly loved children" (Eph. 5:1, HCSB). The word translated as "imitate" can also be translated from the original Greek as "reflect" or "mirror." Paul's meaning is clear: we are to be "mirrors" or "reflections" of God.

Mirrors are not complex—they simply reflect the image of whatever is in front of them. A mirror can take no credit for the image it reflects, just as we can take no credit for the reflection of God that shines through our lives in our relationship with Him. And just as a mirror does not become the thing it reflects, so our calling is not to become a god, but simply to reflect God.

We are called to be reflections.

When people look at our lives, they should see the reflection of the one who created us. However, unless God gives us a distinct picture of what He looks like, we have no idea whether the image our lives reflect is Him or not. The apostle John emphasized our need for God to make Himself accurately known to us:

> "No one has ever seen God, but the one and only Son, who is himself God and is in closest relationship with the Father, has made him known."
>
> - John 1:18, NIV

Revelation: God Reveals

The fact that God makes Himself known to us is explored in the doctrine of revelation. When introducing the doctrine of revelation to my students, I use a game as an illustration. To begin the game, I reach into my desk and hide a random object inside my closed hand. I then invite the students to guess what I'm holding. Typically, I'll throw in the added incentive that any student who correctly guesses the object will earn an automatic "A" for that day's homework.

As the students begin to guess, I stand quietly with my hand balled into a fist, giving no response. Unlike the game "20 Questions," I do not answer with a "yes" or a "no" in response to their guesses. Unlike the game "Hotter or Colder," I don't give hints or clues to guide the students toward the right answer.

At the beginning, students throw out many excited guesses, inspired by the incentive of an easy "A." But as each guess is met by silence, the room falls quiet fairly quickly and students begin to disengage. When I ask why they have given up, they say I was "not playing along," and they were discouraged because they had no idea whether or not they were guessing the correct answer. Unless I interacted with them in the guessing process, they could have no idea whether or not their guesses were correct.

Our relationship with God works in a similar way.

Unless God chooses to reveal Himself to us, we have no way of knowing what He's like . . . and no idea whether or not our ideas are even close.

The doctrine of revelation teaches us that God opens His hand to humanity because He wants us to know and love Him.

Look back at John 1 and reconsider the meaning of the words: "the one and only Son, who is himself God and is in closest relationship with the Father, has made Him known."

God has opened His hand to you and me because He desires us to know and love Him.

Jesus has made God known to us, so we may respond to God with love and live according to our divine design by reflecting His glory. Paul refers to this concept as our "true and proper worship."

> "Therefore, I urge you, brothers and sisters, in view of God's mercy, to offer your bodies as a living sacrifice, holy and pleasing to God—this is your true and proper worship."
>
> - Romans 12:1, NIV

If Jesus hadn't come to Earth to live a human life—fully human, yet also fully the Son of God—we wouldn't have a model of what a perfect reflection of God looks like. We could very quickly lose interest in the pursuit of our purpose, because we'd have no idea if we were headed in the right direction.

Many people's spiritual journeys resemble the type of disengagement that my students experienced while guessing what was hidden in my hand. When people don't have a clear direction and understanding of how to model their lives after God, they often compensate by creating spiritual to-do lists, busying their lives with programs, or patterning their goals after an admired teacher, pastor, or Christian leader. These people begin their journeys with high hopes, noble desires, and great intentions, but they lack clarity about what is supposed to come next. This uncertainty leads to frustration, discouragement, and eventually disengagement.

Smile More, Swear Less?

Sensing we were created for something greater than our own small lives and self-centered desires, we long for something deeper—some significant experience with God. We know instinctively that we are called to do more than achieve perfect church attendance or good grades. Deep inside, we have unsatisfied longings. We know our efforts to increase our spiritual health by measurable increments or to fix specific sin patterns are merely behavior modifications, and not necessarily indicative of a changed heart.

Perhaps you've experienced the perplexity that comes when, after a success, your efforts feel empty—yet your love for God propels you to try harder. Or maybe you've felt the weight of your struggle against sin, but after experiencing failed attempts to fix yourself, you grew weary. You've found yourself wondering:

Does God really expect me to be a *perfect* reflection, or is He just suggesting that as a "best-case scenario"?

Some of us believe God is being cruel by expecting us to accomplish something He knows is humanly impossible. So our spiritual lives stall—either because of the disillusionment that results from choosing a model that has failed us, or because we're tired of a way of life that seems unfulfilling. Often our hearts are in the right place, but our efforts feel like a series of conflicts and contradictions that lack clear direction, focus, or fulfillment.

What we need is for God to clearly reveal His expectations. We need a perfect model to pattern our lives after—a model that will give us the direction we long for.

Some of us are scared. Others are tired. Our previous models have left us feeling worn-out, unsatisfied, and unfulfilled. We are afraid to again face the disappointment and exhaustion of another fruitless attempt, yet our pervasive longing to live out the purpose we were created for won't go away.

Thankfully, God provided the solution we need through the person of His Son, Jesus Christ.

Immediately after saying we are to become "imitators of God, as beloved children," Paul points us to our perfect model in the next verse: we are to live and love "just as Christ" (Eph. 5:1-2, NASB).

Just as Christ

In addition to what general revelation teaches about who God is and how He wants us to live, we also have Jesus Himself as our ultimate example. Ephesians 5:2 reminds us that Jesus is the perfect example of a life that reflects God's glory and is pleasing to God. The author of Hebrews also writes:

"The Son is the radiance of God's glory and the exact representation of his being, sustaining all things by his powerful word. After he had provided purification for sins, he sat down at the right hand of the Majesty in heaven."

- Hebrews 1:3, NIV

Jesus is the "exact representation" of God's being. We should live our lives with Jesus as our example, making it our desire to live just as He lived: in perfect relationship with the Father and in trusting submission to the Father's will. Jesus once explained it to His disciple Philip like this:

"Jesus answered: 'Don't you know me, Philip, even after I have been among you such a long time? Anyone who has seen me has seen the Father. How can you say, "Show us the Father"?'"

- John 14:9, NIV

Jesus is the perfect reflection of the radiance of God's glory.

For us to fulfill God's purpose for our lives, we must imitate the Father just as Jesus did. Jesus is the only role model who will never let us down, because He is both the author and the perfecter of our faith. As such, the writer of the letter to the Hebrews tells us to fix our eyes on Him:

"[F]ixing our eyes on Jesus, the author and perfecter of faith, who for the joy set before him endured the cross, despising the shame, and has sat down at the right hand of the throne of God."

- Hebrews 12:2, NASB

The only catch to the solution of "fixing our eyes on Jesus" is that our understanding of Jesus is certainly incomplete and often flawed. Our culture propagates a very flawed view of Jesus. The result is a distorted, confusing, and inaccurate depiction of the Son of God. Our culture's depiction of Jesus is often less of a reflection of the real Son of God and more an example of the famous saying:

**"God created man in His own image
and then we returned the favor."**

The truth is, any culture that lives to reflect its own values more than to reflect the glory of God cannot give us an accurate reflection of Jesus. The only place where we can be certain the portrait of Jesus matches truth is in the revelation of God in the Bible.

The task of uncovering an accurate understanding of Jesus in the pages of Scripture may seem daunting. Where do we start? Do we begin by making a list of everything Jesus said and did? Do we write every command Jesus gave and carry that list in our pockets until we memorize all of them?

Where do we look to find an answer? Is it God's intention that we memorize every obscure biblical rule or law in order to walk a spiritual tightrope, striving for perfection but motivated by the haunting fear of what happens if we fall off?

What Happens If We Fail?

I'm not sure about you, but the thought of having a relationship with God that's grounded in my own attempts to be perfect and in my fear of failure seems very discouraging and unsustainable. Yet many of our efforts toward spiritual maturity are based on the futile, exhausting idea that we must "do all the right things."

But there is a solution to our problem that is much better than this misguided, self-centered, and ultimately hopeless effort for perfection: a solution centered on Jesus Christ.

God, in His infinite wisdom, mercy, and love, gives us a simple, childlike solution to our dilemma of needing a clear picture of the way He wants us to live.

The explanation for this wonderful solution is explained in the doctrine of the Incarnation. The word "incarnation" has at its root the word *carne*, which literally means "meat" or "flesh." Incarnation is a reference to "God with flesh," and the concept can be found in John 1:14:

> "The Word became flesh, and lived among us. We saw his glory, such glory as of the one and only Son of the Father, full of grace and truth."
>
> - John 1:14, WEB

Incarnation: God with Flesh

This verse gives us an outline of how the Word (Jesus) became flesh (incarnate) and lived among us as a fellow human, so we could see the glory of the Father reflected in our midst.

**Understanding this verse gives us a destination.
Applying this verse gives us direction.**

If we want to see the glory of God the Father, we should look to Jesus. If we want to see the full and complete grace of the Father reflected and perfectly lived out, we should look to Jesus. If we want to become spiritually mature reflections of the Father, we should reflect Jesus. If we want to live in accordance with our divinely appointed purpose, we should reflect Jesus.

Only Jesus is the exact radiance of God's glory. Only Jesus perfectly reflects and defines for us the completeness of God's grace and truth.

Jesus Is Our Perfect Example

In light of this, we should fix our eyes on Jesus and take our cues from Him. Jesus is the perfect reflection of God. He alone is the picture of spiritual maturity. Fixing our eyes on Him and making Him our model, and making His life our standard for a life well-lived, is the only solution to our worn-out efforts.

In our pursuit of knowing Jesus, we should have an attitude like that of the merchant in Jesus' famous parable. He discovered a pearl of great value, and after finding it, he went with joy to sell all he had in order to purchase that pearl (Matt. 13:45-46). We should also take on the attitude of determination displayed by a group of Greeks who would allow nothing to stand in the way of their quest to see Jesus for themselves:

"So these came to Philip . . . and asked him, 'Sir, we wish to see Jesus.'"

- John 12:21, ESV

Knowing Jesus for who He really is (and not the distorted version of Him that our culture, our friends, or even we ourselves have inaccurately portrayed) must become a driving passion in our lives. If we are to accurately live out our purpose to reflect our Creator, we must accurately know and reflect Jesus.

Reflection

1. What ideas or images stood out to you in this chapter?

2. What was encouraging? Why?

3. What was frustrating? Why?

4. Describe how our culture portrays Jesus.

5. How might the image of Jesus projected by culture impact your perspective of Him?

6. Describe how you personally picture Jesus. Does your perspective of Him lean more toward a view of Him inviting you to memorize rules, or is your perspective more similar to the "smile more, swear less" Jesus? Why?

7. How did this chapter challenge your image of Jesus? Explain.

CHAPTER 6

REDEMPTION BY BLOOD

How do we re-embrace our divine calling to reflect the image of God and to realign our lives to God's purpose and will? Is it possible to scrape off all the dried "mud" attached to our lives so the light of Christ and the image of God can shine through? Is it possible to reorient our desires away from discontentment and, instead, accept our divine purpose? How can muddied mirrors become perfected reflections?

In my current position as a Bible teacher at a Christian high school, I am privileged to teach a semester-long class on the life of Christ. On the first day of each new semester, all the students in the class receive a formative assessment designed to uncover some of the questions they would like to answer during the semester. Typically, the top three questions are variations of the following:

1. Why did Jesus have to die?

2. How are the Old and New Testaments connected?

3. What's the deal with the killing of animals in the Old Testament, and how is that connected to Christ's death on the cross?

The first semester I compiled these questions, I was a bit surprised that these were the most frequent responses. Yet, hundreds of students later, these three questions continue to rise to the surface each semester. Perhaps you've asked the same questions yourself.

To find answers, it's easiest to begin by returning to the Genesis account of Adam and Eve—to examine the events immediately following their choice to place their will over God's by eating fruit from the tree of the knowledge of good and evil.

"Then the eyes of both of them were opened, and they realized they were naked; so they sewed fig leaves together and made coverings for themselves."

- Genesis 3:7, NIV

The first observation from verse seven is that Adam and Eve's eyes were "opened" to their need for something to cover themselves. Just a few verses earlier, at the end of chapter two, they'd been described as uncovered and unashamed.

The word "shame" carries many applicable nuances. First, shame is a negative emotion.

Shame connotes feelings of unworthiness, regret, separation, and disgrace.

Immediately after their decision to defy the known will of God by following the course of action they deemed more pleasurable and desirable, Adam and Eve were greeted with the negative emotional consequences of shame and grief.

None of these deeply negative emotions would have been natural parts of Adam and Eve's previous life experience. Created in the image of God and living in harmony with God and with His creation, there had been no reason for them to doubt their significance, purpose, or the meaning of their lives. Yet now they questioned their value for the first time and struggled with a deep sense of unworthiness.

In a single moment, Adam and Eve felt the terrifying impact of the loss of their innocence. They experienced, with deep regret, the consequences of an action that took them outside of the close and trusting relationship with God.

Because of their act of disobedience and defiance against God, Adam and Eve also experienced disgrace and humiliation for the first time. The word "disgrace" means "a loss of respect." Judging by Adam's words in verse 12 (in which he blames Eve for their decision), the loss of respect that occurs between the man and woman is jarring.

To add to the shock overwhelming them, Adam's and Eve's eyes were also opened to their own nakedness. For the first time, they felt a need for a physical covering. Humiliated by this knowledge, they tried to create clothes for themselves.

Adam and Eve put on their new clothes, only to realize their solution was inadequate. As they heard the sound of the Lord God walking toward them, they were painfully aware of their own exposure. Gripped by fear, they hid from God (Gen. 3:8).

Perhaps their reason for hiding was they recognized the insufficiency of their makeshift coverings to hide their nakedness and vulnerability. Perhaps it was also connected to their fear of the inevitable consequence of their disobedience: death. Attached to God's original instructions for them had been the warning that, if they disobeyed God by eating the fruit from the tree of the knowledge of good and evil, they would certainly die.

The apostle Paul would later compare this cause-and-effect relationship between sin and death to the relationship between a worker and his wages when he wrote:

"For the wages of sin is death."
                                            - Romans 6:23a, NIV

Paul's illustration is straightforward for anyone who has worked a paying job. At the end of each pay period, every worker expects to receive the amount of money agreed to in his or her contract. In Adam and Eve's case, their original agreement (contract) was that their disobedience to God's will would result in death.

Paul's brilliant metaphor compares the sense of expectation that workers have toward their deserved wages to the relationship between sin and death. When God gave the nation of Israel the laws that would act as the framework for their religious and social lives, one law in particular stated:

> "The wages of a hired worker shall not remain with you all night until the morning."
> - Leviticus 19:13b, ESV

Have you ever experienced a sinking feeling immediately after making a choice you knew was wrong? That feeling where you know your actions and motives are suddenly completely exposed? When the adrenaline working in your favor during the moments that led up to the bad decision suddenly slams on the brakes? Instead of the euphoria of success, you are gripped with the fear of being caught.

In a similar way, Adam and Eve felt immediate, sickening regret after disobeying God. They knew they were about to receive the agreed-upon wages for their actions, so they felt exposed and afraid.

Hiding from God

Adam and Eve's sense of exposure and their awareness of the impending punishment of death would only have increased as they heard God calling, "Where are you?" Recognizing the futility of his attempts to hide his sin, Adam entered into his first conversation with God from his now-fallen state.

> "[Adam] answered, 'I heard you in the garden, and I was afraid because I was naked; so I hid.'
>
> "And [God] said, 'Who told you that you were naked? Have you eaten from the tree that I commanded you not to eat from?'"
>
> - Genesis 3:10-11, NIV

In a response that would have been abnormal up until that moment, but has since become a common instinct, Adam reacts to this confrontation by deflecting blame away from himself and instead toward his Creator and his wife. By attempting to transfer blame to someone else, Adam was reacting out of his own inability to cover his actions before God. Adam needed a covering. He needed something to make up for (or atone for) his sin.

Adam and Eve knew God had promised a decision to disobey Him would result in death. They were frightened by the futility of their own attempts to place something between them and God.

They were in desperate need of atonement.

So what did God do next?

"The LORD God made garments of skin for Adam and his wife and clothed them."
                                        - Genesis 3:21, NIV

Forbearance

In His forbearance and mercy, God did not cause Adam and Eve to undergo the immediate, terminal consequences of their choice. Instead He took the life of an animal to provide a covering for their sin and nakedness.

This act appeased the justice of God (through the substitutionary death of the animal) and also displayed the love of God by providing a covering for Adam and Eve's exposure. Clothed by the sacrifice that God had provided, Adam and Eve were able to experience reconciliation with their Creator.

After Adam and Eve's disobedience introduced sin and death into the world, God—in His love, mercy, and forbearance—offered a series of substitutions that gave His people a way to be reconciled with Himself.

One of the ways God provided reconciliation was through the sacrificial system under the Law. In addition to daily sacrifices, one particular day each year was designed to be the day on which the sins of the previous year were atoned. On this day, all the people were made clean before God.

> "For on this day shall atonement be made for you to cleanse you. You shall be clean before the LORD from all your sins."
>
> - Leviticus 16:30, ESV

While the sacrificial system under the Law provided an important way for God and His people to be reconciled, the Law made it clear that human effort alone could never remove the fundamental problem of sin. The Law only made people more aware of their sin (see Romans 3:20).

Atonement

The annual Day of Atonement, called *Yom Kippur,* was designed to bring reconciliation between God and His people through a specific process. It was essential to follow every step of the process to the smallest detail, because a failure to do so would leave the sins of the people uncovered. In addition, each step foreshadowed the ultimate act of atonement.

> "Once a year Aaron shall make atonement on its horns. This annual atonement must be made with the blood of the atoning sin offering for the generations to come. It is most holy to the LORD."
>
>   - Exodus 30:10, NIV

Three key elements to the process of the day included the priest, the first sacrifice of propitiation, and a second sacrificial act of expiation (Leviticus 16).

The priest acted as the mediator between the sinful people and the sinless God, whose image they were perverting.

"Propitiation" referred to the diversion of the payment of sin away from the people of God onto an atoning sacrifice.

"Expiation" referred to the cleansing of sin that is made available through a second sacrificial act.

The Priest

Because the human priest was himself unclean, the process of atonement could begin only after the priest completed a process of being made clean before God. After a ritual cleansing and the offering of sacrifices for his own sin and those of his family, the high priest would cast lots over two goats (Lev. 16:8) to determine which of the two goats to sacrifice to the Lord. The Bible and history record that the high priest would use the casting of lots as a way to allow God to determine the outcome of difficult decisions.

The author of Proverbs wrote:

> "The lot is cast into the lap,
>   but its every decision is from the LORD."
>   - Proverbs 16:33, NIV

The casting of lots on the Day of Atonement illustrated God's sovereignty in choosing an acceptable sacrifice as a substitution to cover His people's sins. This substitution of a sinless animal for a guilty, sinful life is an example of propitiation.

The Sacrifice of Propitiation

Propitiation is the diversion of God's righteous judgment away from us and onto God's chosen substitutionary sacrifice. This sacrifice of propitiation was a sacrifice of blood that resulted in the animal's death. This substitution is reminiscent of the first animal that died to provide a covering for Adam and Eve after their initial rebellion against God.

Just as Adam and Eve experienced the forbearance of God through the death of an animal, the blood of the first goat on the Day of Atonement satisfied the penalty for the sins of the people.

> "Then Aaron shall offer the goat on which the lot for the LORD fell, and make it a sin offering."
>
> - Leviticus 16:9, NASB

The Sacrifice of Expiation

After the sin offering was accepted, the high priest would lay both of his hands on the second live goat and confess the sins of the people (Lev. 16:21). This act, known as "imputation," demonstrated the transference of sin from the people onto the second goat. In other words, the sins of the people would be expiated (removed) and the people would be cleansed from their sin. Then this goat, called the "scapegoat," would be led into a remote part of the wilderness several miles outside of the camp.

The goat, bearing the sin of the people, would be set free into the wilderness. This action represented expiation: the cleansing and removal of sin from the people.

Through this process, the priest would make atonement for the entire community of Israel. The sins of the past year would be atoned for through the sacrifice of the first goat. It satisfied the wrath of God by diverting it from the people to the goat. The second sacrifice—the scapegoat released into the wilderness—would remind them that their sins were not only paid for, but completely cleansed and remembered no more.

Daily Reminders

In order for the people of God to re-embrace their divine calling and realign themselves to His divine design for their lives, they need to be cleansed. During the era of the Old Testament, this cleansing was accomplished through animal sacrifices: both on the annual Day of Atonement (as described previously) and also on a smaller scale throughout the year. The people of Israel were expected to offer sacrifices regularly. Each sacrifice was a reminder of their constant struggle against sin and their need for God's mercy and atonement. We would still need to offer that type of sacrifice to this day—if not for the permanent solution God offered just under 2,000 years ago.

God's Perfect Design

One of the most incredible aspects of God's perfect design is that He demonstrated His love for us by sending us His Son. Jesus came in order to become a human being and to be our perfect priest, our perfect sacrifice, and our perfect scapegoat. While we were still His enemies, Jesus became our perfect and final atonement on the cross.

"But God demonstrates his own love for us in this: While we were still sinners, Christ died for us."

- Romans 5:8, NIV

God's Perfect Priest

One of the most important figures in the Old Testament sacrificial system was the high priest, who acted as the mediator between the sinful people and their holy God.

But there was a problem: human priests were imperfect. Therefore it was necessary for a priest to first offer a sacrifice on his own behalf. This would ensure a right standing before God *before* he could offer sacrifices on behalf of the people. The result, according to the author of Hebrews, was that even though the system served a temporary purpose, it was incomplete and imperfect.

To achieve a permanent solution, there needed to be a perfect priest who could offer a perfect sacrifice. Someone who wouldn't need to offer sacrifices day after day—first for his own sin and then for the sin of the people (Heb. 7:27).

Jesus is that perfect priest.

"For this reason he [Jesus] had to be made like them, fully human in every way, in order that he might become a merciful and faithful high priest in service to God, and that he might make atonement for the sins of the people."

- Hebrews 2:17, NIV

In chapter 10, the writer of Hebrews adds that in spite of serving the Lord by offering the same sacrifices day after day, the original priesthood and sacrificial system were never designed as a permanent solution for our sin (Heb. 10:2, 11). Instead, they were a foreshadowing of the perfect High Priest and His permanent sacrificial offering (Heb. 10:10, 12).

God's Perfect Sacrifice

In addition to a perfect high priest, a perfect and permanent sacrifice was needed:

"God presented Christ as a sacrifice of atonement, through the shedding of his blood—to be received by faith. He did this to demonstrate his righteousness, because in his forbearance he had left the sins committed beforehand unpunished."

- Romans 3:25, NIV

Christ became our perfect High Priest, as well as our perfect sacrifice to replace the imperfect system. The writer of Hebrews combines these concepts when he writes:

"Consequently, when Christ came into the world, he said,

"'Sacrifices and offerings you have not desired,
    but a body have you prepared for me;
in burnt offerings and sin offerings
    you have taken no pleasure.
Then I said, 'Behold, I have come to do your will, O God, as it is written of me in the scroll of the book.'
"When he said above, 'You have neither desired nor taken pleasure in sacrifices and offerings and burnt offerings and sin offerings' (these are offered according to the law), then he added, 'Behold, I have come to do your will.' He does away with the first in order to establish the second. And by that will we have been sanctified through the offering of the body of Jesus Christ once for all."
                                          - Hebrews 10:5-10, ESV

As we see all of these pieces falling into place in God's perfect design, we should not miss the fact that, tucked into the middle of Hebrews 10, these words of Christ are repeated twice, as if to ensure we don't overlook their significance:

"Behold, I have come to do your will."
> - Hebrews 10:7, 9, ESV

These words of Christ—our perfect priest and perfect sacrifice—should echo in our ears as an example of the attitude we should have toward God. It is exactly the opposite of Adam and Eve's attitude when they defied God's will in the Garden of Eden.

God's Perfect Reflection

Jesus, the perfect High Priest, offered the perfect sacrifice of atonement by the shedding of His sinless blood. He cleanses us from our sin—from our choice to abandon the will of God. Through it all, Jesus is a perfect example of obedience to the Father's will. Paul sums up this concept in Romans 5:

> "For as by the one man's disobedience the many were made sinners, so by the one man's obedience the many will be made righteous."
> - Romans 5:19, ESV

God's Perfect Result

But while it is the blood of Christ that cleanses us of sin, it is the resurrection of Christ from the dead that completes the good news of the gospel message and brings us true life (1 John 1:7).

> "For since by a man came death, by a man also came the resurrection of the dead. For as in Adam all die, so also in Christ all will be made alive."
> - 1 Corinthians 15:21-22, NASB

Remember the three questions mentioned at the beginning of this chapter?

1. Why did Jesus have to die?

2. How are the Old and New Testaments connected?

3. What's the deal with the killing of animals in the Old Testament, and how are they connected to Christ's death on the cross?

Let's respond to these questions, but in reverse order.

#3: What's the deal with the killing of animals in the Old Testament, and how are they connected to Christ's death on the cross?

The sacrifice of animals during the Old Testament era was an important but temporary part of God's plan. He designed this system to point toward the future: the perfect substitutionary atonement that His Son, Jesus, would later bring to completion.

#2: How are the Old and New Testaments connected?

The incomplete system of offerings designed to deal with sin during the Old Testament era was a daily, weekly, and yearly reminder of the people's bondage to sin and their inability to deal with it apart from God's grace. Ultimately, God would demonstrate His love toward the world through the life of His Son, Jesus Christ.

Through His life, death, and resurrection, Christ demonstrated God's love for us by taking our sin upon Himself, so that the wrath of God would be diverted away from us and onto Himself instead. His death on the cross is a permanent payment for the sins of the world. Jesus is also our model of submission of our own will to the Father's will. He is the perfect example for us to model our lives after.

> "For you have been called for this purpose, since Christ also suffered for you, leaving you an example for you to follow in His steps."
>
> - 1 Peter 2:21, NASB

#1: Why did Jesus have to die?

Jesus answered this question Himself:

> "If anyone serves me, he must follow me; and where I am, there will my servant be also. If anyone serves me, the Father will honor him.
>
> "Now is my soul troubled. And what shall I say? 'Father, save me from this hour'? *But for this purpose I have come to this hour.*"
>
> - John 12:26-27, ESV (italics mine)

Jesus died to fulfill the purposes of the Father. In doing so, He not only provided the perfect atonement to cover the sins of the world, but also provided us with a perfect picture of the love and grace of God.

In Genesis 3, after Adam and Eve gathered their fig leaves to cover their sin, they realized the incompleteness of their attempts. As a result, they hid from God in fear.

**It was not until God provided a covering of
His own through an act of grace that they could
step out of hiding and back into His presence.**

Jesus Is Our Substitution

Jesus willingly takes our place. He is our sacrifice of atonement for the sins we've committed against God. His death and resurrection provide permanent covering for our sins.

> "In him we have redemption through his blood, the forgiveness of sins, in accordance with the riches of God's grace that he lavished on us. With all wisdom and understanding . . ."
>
> - Ephesians 1:7-8, NIV

Pay close attention to the words Paul uses in these verses. The word "redemption" conveys the idea that we are being purchased, or "bought back."

**God, through Jesus, has exchanged (redeemed)
you from your own rebellious attempts to sit on
the throne of your own life and reflect your
own image instead of the image of God.**

Jesus has offered us His covering with the opportunity to be completely forgiven. As a result, you can be cleansed from the dirt and grime of sin that has been caked onto the mirror of your life. You can be freed to experience a new life.

> "Let us walk properly as in the daytime, not in orgies and drunkenness, not in sexual immorality and sensuality, not in quarreling and jealousy. But put on the Lord Jesus Christ, and make no provision for the flesh, to gratify its desires."
>
> — Romans 13:13-14, ESV

> "[F]or all of you who were baptized into Christ have clothed yourselves with Christ."
>
> — Galatians 3:27, NIV

> "[T]o put off your old self, which belongs to your former manner of life and is corrupt through deceitful desires, and to be renewed in the spirit of your minds, and to put on the new self, created after the likeness of God in true righteousness and holiness."
>
> — Ephesians 4:22-24, ESV

> "Do not lie to one another, seeing that you have put off the old self with its practices and have put on the new self, which is being renewed in knowledge after the image of its creator."
>
> — Colossians 3:9-10, ESV

In light of this, how do we re-embrace our divine calling and realign ourselves to accomplish God's purpose of reflecting His image and will through our lives?

Why would we not immediately cease our feeble attempts to cover our own sin and accept God's perfect sacrifice and perfect covering through His gracious act of atonement?

The reality is that you and I could never be good enough on our own to earn God's forgiveness.

The theological term for the removal of our sin before God is "justification." Justification is not made possible by our efforts, but by God's grace.

The prophet Isaiah calls our good deeds "filthy rags."

> "All of us have become like one who is unclean,
>   and all our righteous acts are like filthy rags;
> we all shrivel up like a leaf,
>   and like the wind our sins sweep us away."
>   - Isaiah 64:6, NIV

Any continued attempts to be "good enough" on our own, or to cover our sins with our good behavior, are just as futile as Adam and Eve trying to hide their nakedness with fig leaves before a holy and righteous God. It's simply not possible for us to ever do enough good works to cover our sin. It's not possible for us to scrape off all the mud and grime from our lives in order for the reflection of Christ to shine through.

Paul brings all these concepts and illustrations together in a letter he wrote to a young pastor named Titus.

> "[H]e [God] saved us, not because of righteous things we had done, but because of his mercy. He saved us through the washing of rebirth and renewal by the Holy Spirit, whom he poured out on us generously through Jesus Christ our Savior, so that, having been justified by his grace, we might become heirs having the hope of eternal life."
>
> - Titus 3:5-7, NIV

Lavish Love

Notice that the overwhelming love of God is described with the words "poured out on us generously." The only way we can reorient our desires away from ourselves and toward God is by submitting our will to God's will. We must put off our old selves and put on Christ.

**In God's divine plan, Christ's substitution
is the only solution for "muddied mirrors"
to become perfected reflections.**

Our journey must begin by accepting the gift of justification, offered through the lavish grace He pours out for us through the atoning work of Jesus Christ.

What Then Is Our Response?

Perhaps the only acceptable response is to take our eyes off our own feeble attempts to live in God's divine purpose based on our own good works. We should follow Paul's admonition to the church in Corinth:

> "Examine yourselves, to see whether you are in the faith. Test yourselves. Or do you not realize this about yourselves, that Jesus Christ is in you?—unless indeed you fail to meet the test!"
> - 2 Corinthians 13:5, ESV

An Invitation to Examine Yourself

In the third chapter of the Gospel of John, Jesus talks with a religious leader who has spent his entire life trying to reach God by obeying the law as best he could. This man,

Nicodemus, came to Jesus because in spite of his best attempts, he sensed that his own efforts would never lead him to a right relationship with God. Jesus tells Nicodemus that he must be "born again." This suggestion startles Nicodemus.

> "Jesus answered him, 'Most certainly, I tell you, unless one is born anew, he can't see God's Kingdom.'
>
> "Nicodemus said to him, 'How can a man be born when he is old? Can he enter a second time into his mother's womb, and be born?'"
>
> - John 3:3-4, WEB

In the next few verses, Jesus and Nicodemus talk back and forth while Jesus explains that everyone experiences a physical birth, but only a spiritual rebirth will place a person in a right relationship with God. When he asks Jesus to explain, Jesus responds:

> "For God so loved the world, that he gave his one and only Son, that whoever believes in him should not perish, but have eternal life. For God didn't send his Son into the world to judge the world, but that the world should be saved through him. He who believes in him is not judged. He who doesn't believe has been judged already, because he has not believed in the name of the one and only Son of God."
>
> - John 3:16-18, WEB

The apostle Paul would later explain to the early church in Rome that the gift of God is the substitutionary payment of Jesus' life, which results in the gift of right-standing and eternal life with God. But like any gift, this gift cannot only be given—it must also be received.

One of the ways to understand this concept of substitution and rebirth is by using the acronym "ABC." These letters stand for "Admit," "Believe," and "Confess."

A. Admit you are a sinner and no amount of good works on your part will ever fix you. The Bible says:

> "[F]or all have sinned, and fall short of the glory of God."
>
> - Romans 3:23, WEB

> "For the wages of sin is death."
>
> - Romans 6:23a, WEB

> "[N]ot by works of righteousness, which we did ourselves, but according to his mercy, he saved us."
>
> - Titus 3:5a, WEB

Personal Reflection: Do I acknowledge that I have stepped away from God's design for my life and have disregarded God's will, preferring my own desires and priorities?

B. Believe that Jesus is the Son of God, that He lived a perfect human life, that He offered His life as a payment for your sin, and that He rose again from the dead to set you free from the power of sin and death.

> "'He committed no sin,
>   and no deceit was found in his mouth.'

> "When they hurled their insults at him, he did not retaliate; when he suffered, he made no threats. Instead, he entrusted himself to him who judges justly. 'He himself bore our sins' in his body on the cross, so that we might die to sins and live for righteousness; 'by his wounds you have been healed.'"
>
> - 1 Peter 2:22-24, NIV

> "For what I received I passed on to you as of first importance: that Christ died for our sins according to the Scriptures, that he was buried, that he was raised on the third day according to the Scriptures, and that he appeared to Cephas, and then to the Twelve."
>
> - 1 Corinthians 15:3-5, NIV

> "For it is by grace you have been saved, through faith—and this is not from yourselves, it is the gift of God—not by works, so that no one can boast."
>
> - Ephesians 2:8-9, NIV

Personal Reflection: Do I believe that Jesus is the Son of God, that He lived a perfect life, that He offered His life as a payment for my sin, and then rose again from the dead to set me free from the power of sin and death?

C. Change your mind about whose will to follow, and confess your faith in Jesus as your Savior and Lord, receiving His gift of atonement and forgiveness.

> "If you declare with your mouth, 'Jesus is Lord,' and believe in your heart that God raised him from the dead, you will be saved. For it is with your heart that you believe and are justified, and it is with your mouth that you profess your faith and are saved. As Scripture says, 'Anyone who believes in him will never be put to shame.'"
>
> - Romans 10:9-11, NIV

Personal Reflection: Have I (or will I) change my mind about whose will to follow? Have I (or will I) confess my faith in Jesus as my Savior and Lord, receiving His gift of forgiveness for my sin and rebellion against Him?

Do Those Truths Reflect Where You Are Now?

Have you ever expressed your thoughts to God?

The word "prayer" means the activity of talking with God.

There is nothing magical or mystical about prayer. There is nothing you need to memorize or words you have to repeat in order to talk with God. Because God invites us to experience a relationship with Him, He also invites us to simply speak to Him like we would to a friend.

If this is one of your first times talking with God through prayer, you may want to write your words in the spaces following the prompts on this page and the next.

Talk with Him about how you understand your sin and your need for a Savior.

Talk with Him about what Jesus did on the cross and how He offered His life as a substitute for yours. Then ask God to forgive you for replacing His design and will for your life with your own design.

Talk with Him and invite Him to take His rightful place as the one who is leading and directing your life.

God's Promise to You

The Bible promises that for those who confess their sins to God, He is faithful to hear and to forgive:

> "If we confess our sins, he is faithful and just and will forgive us our sins and purify us from all unrighteousness."
>
> - 1 John 1:9, NIV

Next Steps

If you are going through this book with a friend or a small group and have made a decision to accept Christ's gift of forgiveness, be sure to share your decision with the members of your group.

If you are reading this on your own, I encourage you to find a friend you know is a follower of Jesus and talk about your decision or questions with them.

You can also visit ChristCenteredDiscipleship.com, where you will find resources and encouragement for the next steps in your journey of learning who Jesus is and how to reflect Him in every area of your life.

My Next Steps

What next steps will I take?

Who will I tell?

Reflection

1. What ideas or images stood out to you in this chapter?

2. What was encouraging? Why?

3. What was frustrating? Why?

4. What questions do you have?

5. Have you ever tried hiding from God like Adam and Eve did? What was the result?

6. What are your thoughts about how God designed the system of sacrifices to point toward Jesus, who would become our ultimate sacrifice?

7. How does understanding the system of sacrifices change your perspective of God? How does it change your perspective of Jesus?

8. After reading this chapter, has Jesus become more of a hero in your mind? Why or why not?

9. If you were to examine yourself right now, would you say you are trying to create your own covering for your sin, or have you accepted Christ's atonement covering? Explain your answer.

CHAPTER 7

THE FULLNESS
OF CHRIST

We were created to reflect the image and glory of God, but we rebelled against this design. We questioned God's motivation and intentions, and, instead of trusting His design, we followed other paths: ways of life that seemed safer, smarter, more fulfilling, more desirable.

But we were wrong to reject God's design. Our attempts to restore our relationship with God through good behavior or good intentions still leave us pitifully exposed. On their own, these acts of righteousness can only turn the hardened dirt of our lives into a muddy mess: that is, until Christ—the Son of God, who changed His role from our Creator to become our Redeemer—offered us the gift of life through His death and resurrection (1 Cor. 15:3-4). Jesus gives us the opportunity to be clothed in His righteousness and to fulfill our true purpose by reflecting God through our lives. This is the good news of the gospel message.

We Are God's Masterpiece

Our lives bear witness to the glory of God through the grace of God at work in our lives through the act of salvation. But how is the message of the gospel lived out to completion on a daily basis?

The apostle Paul, inspired by the Spirit of God, wrote:

> "For we are God's handiwork [*poiema*], created in Christ Jesus to do good works, which God prepared in advance for us to do."
> - Ephesians 2:10, NIV (adapted)

In the first nine verses of this chapter, Paul writes that God has graciously redeemed those who were previously lost. In verse 10, he tells those redeemed people that they are God's *poiema* (pronounced "poy'-ay-mah")—His masterpiece.

If you've been redeemed by Christ, you are His handiwork. You are artfully designed by Him!

Elsewhere, Paul explains that God's handiwork in creation reveals His eternal power and divine nature:

> "For since the creation of the world God's invisible qualities—his eternal power and divine nature—have been clearly seen, being understood from what has been made, so that people are without excuse."
>
> - Romans 1:20, NIV

In the passage from Ephesians, Paul writes that those of us who are reborn are likewise made to display the eternal power and divine nature of our Creator, Jesus Christ, through our lives. That is our work. That is our purpose. It is for His purpose, for His design, and to reflect His glory that our Creator handcrafted each one of us. But how should this message shape our daily lives?

How do we live in a way that accurately reflects God and His glory in every area of life?

In Ephesians 5, the apostle Paul writes to the early Christian church. He calls these believers back to their divine purpose—to be reflections of God. Paul reminds them that they are beloved children of the Father, and he exhorts them to "walk in the way of love." Then he reminds them that their perfect model of love is Jesus Christ, who submitted His will to that of the Father in the second garden.

The Second Garden

The second battle that took place in the Bible was in the Garden of Gethsemane. It was in the second garden, only hours before Jesus would face His torturous death on a cross, that He spoke these words to the Father:

> "My Father, if it is not possible for this cup to be taken away unless I drink it, may your will be done."
> - Matthew 26:42b, NIV

As we reflect on these words of Christ, we must make several observations.

A Very Real Choice

Christ faced legitimate temptation while obeying the will of the Father and while anticipating the pain and shame of the cross (Heb. 12:2b).

The gospel writer John describes the depth to which Christ understood the significance of His choice: either to submit in trusting obedience to the Father's will or to disregard the Father's will to avoid the torment of the cross.

> "Now my soul is troubled, and what shall I say? 'Father, save me from this hour'? No, it was for this very reason I came to this hour. Father, glorify your name!"
>
> - John 12:27-28a, NIV

The gospel writer Luke records that Christ suffered such anguish over the tension between His desire to submit to the will of the Father and His desire to avoid the cross that His sweat was like drops of blood.

> "And being in anguish, he [Jesus] prayed more earnestly, and his sweat was like drops of blood falling to the ground."
>
> - Luke 22:44, NIV

The battle of wills in this second garden is the antithesis of Adam and Eve's choice in the first garden to follow their own desire, instead of trusting God's way.

Rather than seeking His own comfort or glory, Jesus humbled Himself to the will of the Father. Jesus is a perfect reflection of God's love.

In his letter to the Philippian church, Paul explained it like this:

> "And being found in appearance as a man,
> he [Jesus] humbled himself
> by becoming obedient to death—
> even death on a cross!"
> - Philippians 2:8, NIV

In His Own Words

Matthew 26 records the words spoken by Jesus in the Garden of Gethsemane, as He prepared Himself to accomplish the will of the Father by sacrificing His life on the cross.

> "Going a little farther, he fell with his face to the ground and prayed, 'My Father, if it is possible, may this cup be taken from me. Yet not as I will, but as you will.'"
> - Matthew 26:39, NIV

Your Will Be Done

Note the similarity between Jesus' words in this prayer and the words He used when teaching His disciples how to speak to the Father through prayer. While Jesus was teaching His disciples to pray, He said:

"[Y]our kingdom come,
your will be done,
on earth as it is in heaven."

- Matthew 6:10, NIV

In the face of excruciating pain and the cost of His life: Jesus practiced what He preached. He modeled a life that reflected the will of the Father and demonstrated God's design by submitting His life to the will of the Father. Listen to what He says...

"No one takes it from me, but I lay it down of my own accord. I have authority to lay it down, and I have authority to take it up again. This charge I have received from my Father."

- John 10:18, ESV

The Model for Maturity

To ensure there is no question in our minds about God's desire and expectation for us to move beyond spiritual rebirth into spiritual maturity, Paul clarifies this principle when he writes:

"[U]ntil we all attain to the unity of the faith and of the knowledge of the Son of God, to mature manhood, to the measure of the stature of the fullness of Christ."

- Ephesians 4:13, NIV

The word "attain" used in this verse means to "reach, achieve, and accomplish."

The application is that we are to imitate God, just as Christ did, and to become mature, defined as reflecting the "whole measure of the fullness of Christ."

The Fullness of Jesus

Understanding that Jesus is our definition and model for spiritual maturity provides us with clarity, direction, and hope.

No longer is it up to us to define our own models for perfection. Jesus is our model.

No longer is it up to us to define maturity. Jesus is our definition of maturity. No longer is it up to us to search for purpose or meaning in life. Reflecting the glory of our Creator is the purpose for which you and I were designed.

He invites each of us to follow Him on the path toward becoming perfect reflections of Himself for the purpose of participating in the mission that He created us to be a part of.

When we live in our purpose to reflect Jesus and follow His example to glorify God by submitting to His will for the glory of the Father, then we return to our original design and rediscover the eternal meaning to our temporary lives. When we discover God's design for our lives, we find true purpose. When we accept Christ's invitation to follow Him and learn to imitate Him, we discover real direction.

Receiving the gift of forgiveness is just the beginning.

Following Christ and learning to trust and reflect Him in every area of life deepen our understanding of our specific role in the eternal plan and mission of God. As we learn to follow Christ and respond to His invitations to follow Him into new areas we will grow in understanding and confidence in our new relationship.

The Fullness of Jesus

Accepting Christ's gracious gift of forgiveness and returning to a right relationship with Him are only the first steps of God's design for your life. You were created to reflect God, and you are invited to follow Jesus through the process of being transformed to reflect less of yourself and more of Him.

147

Jesus invites you to become His imitator. Just as life outside of God's design is meaningless, so life apart from Him leads to confusion and discouragement.

Respond: Christ-Centered Discipleship

In step two of the Christ-Centered Discipleship series, you'll learn to identify and respond to six specific invitations that Christ uses to guide you toward spiritual maturity. Understanding these invitations will guard you from the landmines of spiritual busyness and spiritual idleness. They'll also equip you to identify your personal spiritual needs and the obstacles to growth you can expect along your journey.

As you learn to identify and apply Jesus' words, you'll gain the clarity, confidence, and direction to live out your divine purpose and design.

Reflection

1. What ideas or images stood out to you in this chapter?

2. What was encouraging? Why?

3. What was frustrating? Why?

4. What questions do you have?

NOTES

ChristCenteredDiscipleship.com

Visit us online for companion resources designed to equip you to take your next step toward reflecting Christ in your circles of influence.

60012652R00093

Made in the USA
Charleston, SC
23 August 2016